PLAN AHEAD

Important Questions (and Answers) Regarding Long-Term Care Insurance

Babs W. Hart

CONTENTS

ACKNOWLEDGEMENTS

This book would not be in your hands today without a lot of help. Although I love the subject and am passionate about people understanding what they purchase in a long-term care insurance contract, it is difficult for me to slow down enough to put the ideas and concepts that you will read in this book on paper.

My sincere appreciation goes to Bill Pomakoy who is the Vice President of Marketing for LTC Consultants, LLC. Bill has been quite amazing in this process; early in the development of this book I made a radical change in the direction and content. Bill graciously has made the adjustments and has given me the support I needed to complete the project. Bill, thanks for not giving up on me.

I could not possibly write a book without acknowledging the impact that my father, **Stewart Welch, Jr.**, has made on my life. Dad turned 96 this past September and continues to go to the office everyday as he has for over 70 years. It is because of Dad that I started in the insurance industry over 22 years ago. He has always taught me the importance of putting the client first. He is also my best referral source because he believes in the importance of long-term care insurance. Hardly a day goes by that he is not calling me with the name of someone that he has spoken to about what he calls "extended care". He and my Mom have given me the love and foundation that has enabled me to be successful.

My brother, Stewart Welch, III; what an amazing guy! He is so like my Dad in so many ways; the epitome of integrity with a heart that genuinely cares for the wellbeing of his friends and clients. Stewart is a nationally recognized financial advisor who is widely quoted in the press. Stewart's company, The Welch Group, LLC, is a fee-only, wealth management advisory firm in Birmingham, Alabama. Stewart has written six books in his areas of expertise. He and his dear wife, Kathie, have always been a source of encouragement.

This book would not have been written without my clients. My goal has always been to educate, educate, educate! It is so important to understand long-term care insurance before you purchase; there is a learning curve! Over the last twenty plus years it has been your questions and more importantly the questions that you did not know you should ask that has prompted this effort.

This acknowledgement may seem silly to you, but it's the game of tennis! When I could not focus any longer I knew it was time to get up a game of doubles and just try to connect with the yellow ball that was coming across the net. I always leave the court renewed, whether I win or lose (more renewed when I win).

Finally, and in saving the best acknowledgement for last, my husband, Robert; I had no idea 42 years ago when he asked and I said yes to a lifetime together what a compassionate, loving, unique, wonderful person would be my partner. Together we have tried to serve our Lord and Savior, Jesus Christ; in that effort, Robert has been my example of what it means to "walk the walk".

Robert has read and re-read every word of this book, made countless changes and suggestions. He is patient and supportive and has a talent for sentence composition that has been invaluable.

FORWARD

CONGRATULATIONS for making the investment in your financial future by reading <u>Plan Ahead</u> by Babs W. Hart. I have known Babs personally and professionally for about 20 years, and she is a leading expert in helping people plan for chronic illness or long-term health care. During these 20 years, I have been impressed by her relentless pursuit of always putting her clients' best interests first. She is a gifted advocate in helping her clients achieve financial security and prosperity.

What impresses me most about Babs is her complete dedication to integrity. She is committed to living a life that is consistent with her personal faith centered on her Christian values. Many people love to speak of their values; Babs chooses to speak volumes without having to open her mouth.

This book is an objective place for you to find information that will assist in your planning for the future. Reading it should help foster good education on this topic so that your loved ones and you can make wise decisions. It was a great decision to obtain a copy of this book. I hope you will make an even better decision by reading it, making notes, and telling your friends about it. Good Reading.

Andrew S. Martin
President, First Protective

Discussing long-term care needs with our clients has increased dramatically in recent years. As a firm we made the decision that to better serve our clients we needed to have a strategic alliance with someone who had the heart of a teacher, who was independent, and who was truly passionate about helping families protect their long-term care needs. There was only one choice in our minds and that was Babs Hart. She, in my opinion, defines the word professional, and is the only person we feel comfortable referring our clients to for this important area of their personal financial program.

William A. B. Dowell (Bill)
Vision Financial Group, Inc
4908 Cahaba River Road, Suite 104
Birmingham, Alabama 35243
205-970-4909
800-374-4332

www.vision-financialgroup.com
email- bdowell@vision-financialgroup.com

Bill Dowell is a Registered Representative of ProEquities, Inc., A Registered Broker-Dealer, Member FINRA & SIPC. Bill is not affiliated with ProEquities, Inc.

Bill is Series 6 licensed in the states of AL,CA, CO,FL,GA,IL,LA,MS,NC,TN, and TX

Several years ago I listened to the end of a radio interview, regarding retirement planning for women. The professional, being interviewed, impressed me as she fielded complicated questions about relevant retirement concerns. She demonstrated a solid ability to communicate concepts in an area that I considered very interesting - my future. I wanted to hear more and I imagined that every female I knew would profit from this knowledge.

Babs did a presentation about retirement planning at a seminar at our church. The information she gave us was so compelling that I made an appointment for her to meet with my husband and myself to discuss long-term care insurance. When we began to consider the financial impact of needing long term care services, we decided that owning long term care insurance was the right decision for us.

We want to stay in our home and receive care for as long as possible, and we want to ensure that the resources and all options stay open to us. We enjoyed working with Babs because she carefully explained all the 'moving parts' that impact the benefit and the premium. With the information she provided, we were able to decide on the best plan at a premium we are comfortable paying.

In the years since we bought long-term care insurance from Babs, we have had questions come up and have always felt comfortable calling her. Babs took time to carefully explain the product to us in the beginning and is available now whenever we have questions. That is comforting. Over the years, what began as an inquiry into long-term care insurance for retirement planning has developed into a firm friendship.

~Elizabeth Frazier

Registered Nurse, Case Manager, Health Educator

INTRODUCTION

"Having adequate long-term care insurance is the single most influential determinant of whether an individual will have a financially secure retirement."

~ A study conducted by the Employee Benefit Research Institute -2/10/04)

I HAVE WORKED in the area of long-term care insurance for over twenty years, and have talked with individuals from all across the country. It has been my observation that the reason people procrastinate in making a decision about long-term care insurance is that they don't know the right questions to ask. Good decisions are based largely on one's understanding of a subject and the knowledge of what questions to ask to gain that understanding. I wrote this book to give you those important questions (and answers) related to long-term care insurance so you will be able to make an informed decision for your family and yourself.

If you don't own a long-term care plan, you have one by **default**. You are relying on your own assets and investments, your family and extended family, or the government to take care of you when you become unable to care for yourself—and that means limited choices!

I urge you to use this book as a resource for educating yourself about the issues related to "living too long", so you can determine if this benefit should be part of your complete financial plan.

HOW TO USE THIS BOOK

Read this book with a pen and paper in hand.

Start with Question 1, and as you read, write down any questions that come to mind. Continue this as you read each question so that, in addition to the questions I view as important, you will be prepared with your own questions. As you read, carefully consider not only your spouse and yourself but your dependents and siblings as well because your decisions will impact all those close to you.

Although this book is designed to help you start thinking about long-term care services, it is not a comprehensive guide. Consult your state's insurance department or a trusted agent about specific features or benefits.

Babs W. Hart
The Hart Insurance Group, Inc.
600 Luckie Drive, Suite 200
Birmingham, AL 35223
205-345-7668
www.HartInsuranceGroup.com

CHAPTER 1

IT COULD HAVE BEEN DIFFERENT

Most of us are affected in some way by long-term care needs, and I am no exception. About fifteen years ago my father-in-law needed heart by-pass surgery. He knew by having the surgery he was taking a risk. At first, he thought he would go without the surgery, but he changed his mind. Hindsight would have dictated another choice. He had the surgery and his life, as well as that of the family, was forever different than the previous 85 years. He and my mother in law lived in a beautiful retirement community in Florida. They had actually owned long-term care insurance, but about three years earlier had decided that on their fixed income they would rather spend that money elsewhere. They never mentioned that decision to their son or me.

Often, when one person in a marriage requires extended health care, the healthy spouse may live long past the one needing the care. Because this situation can deplete resources for the surviving spouse, it is imperative that you be conscientious in preserving as much of your financial resources as possible *while* doing everything possible for the loved one needing services. Families are dealing with these issues every day and it is tough financially, emotionally and physically.

It was tough on "Nana". My father-in-law called her at all hours of the day and night because he was unaware of the time. 'Nana' responded by getting out of bed and going down the elevator to the nursing facility that was located on the first floor. This went on for months until she collapsed. When her physician told her she could no longer live alone, she moved to live with us—some 600 miles from the man with whom she had shared more than 60 years of her life.

Over a period of about nine months she gradually regained her strength. About a year later, we were able to move my father- in- law to a facility nearby where he lived for about a month and then passed away. Along with my father-in-law a large part of their wealth had also "passed away" in medical expenses. So much of this stress can and should be avoided. Facing failing health and dying issues are significant enough without adding the stress of having to make tough financial issues.

So how can it be different?

1. If you own long-term care insurance, do everything you can to keep it.
2. Inform your kids if you are thinking about dropping coverage you have; they may want to pay those premiums for you.
3. If you do not own long-term care insurance, consider the options that the insurance industry has available as solutions to a chronic illness or extended health care cost.
4. Use a strong, reputable company through a knowledgeable insurance professional.

Think about it—not owning long-term care insurance is like owning a home without fire and homeowners insurance or a vehicle without automobile insurance. Imagine going to the hospital without health insurance; even if you have the resources to pay the bill out of pocket, there is tremendous peace of mind knowing that you don't have to! Statistically, your chances of needing long-term healthcare are much greater than that of having a fire in the home (1 in 1,200), of being in an automobile accident (1 in 240), or of being hospitalized (1 in 30). Your odds of needing extended healthcare and/or chronic illness insurance are approximately 70% for women and 30% for men. In other words, you have a significant chance of needing some type of long-term healthcare in your lifetime.

In the following chapters, you will find ten questions (and answers) I consider important in learning about long-term care insurance.

If Only My Parents had LTC Insurance

I believe long-term care insurance is extremely important today because healthcare costs continue to escalate. With all the baby-boomers entering their senior years or retiring healthcare costs and issues will only become more acute and expensive during the next 20 years. Both of my parents were very sick at the same time. Ig they had owned long-term care insurance, it would have been much less stressful on my sister and me, both from an emotional and a financial perspective. All of their saving were used for their healthcare during those two years. I worried constantly about the expenses of keeping them in a nursing home and an assisted-living facility, not to mention the hospital bills and pharmaceutical bills for my mother.

I purchased long-term care insurance for my husband and me within two or three months of my parents' deaths, which were just eight months apart. I did not want my daughter to have that same experience with my husband or me since she is our only child. I have been pleased with our purchase of long-term care insurance. I liked working with Babs because she was very honest and upfront about all aspects of the coverage and her knowledge helped me choose the best plan for us. I feel very secure headed into my senior years with this LTC insurance plan and in knowing that we won't be a burden to my daughter. This is a huge comfort.
~ Pam Penick

Notes & Questions:

_____

_____

_____

_____

_____

_____

_____

_____

_____

_____

_____

_____

_____

_____

_____

_____

_____

_____

_____

_____

_____

_____

CHAPTER 2

QUESTION 1: WHAT MAKES LONG-TERM CARE A FAMILY ISSUE?

 Long-term health care has become a critical family issue because we are living longer due to revolutionary advances in medicine. Cardiovascular disease is no longer the killer it once was and cancer deaths are continuing to decline. Medical breakthroughs are impacting diseases such as diabetes and research related to Alzheimer's disease is likely to further the likelihood of a long life, but not necessarily with good health.

According to a recent study conducted by the USC Leonard D Schaeffer Center of Health and Policy Economics (http://healthpolicy.usc.edu) found the following:

- From 2010 to 2050, the number of individuals aged 70+ with Alzheimer's will increase by 153% percent, from 3.6 to 9.1 million.

- Annual per-person costs of the disease were $71,000, in 2010, which is expected to double by 2050.

- Medicare and Medicaid currently bear 75 percent of the costs of the disease.

Because of the progressive nature of Alzheimer's, patients eventually need care 24 hours a day which is usually provided in a facility. Prior to the patient being in a facility, family members often need to take time off work to be the caregiver.

So often, when the focus is on the person needing care, the needs of the caregiver are overlooked. In many situations, care-giving responsibilities are not distributed evenly among family members. One family member may live close enough to assume all or most of the care-giving. Another may be able to contribute financially to the need of the care recipient. Still others may not be willing or able to share the mounting cost of care or the duties related to being a caregiver.

I remember one family where the daughters lived in the city with the ailing parent and were caring for her needs often to the detriment of their own families. The son lived in California and would fly home a couple of times a years with only complaints of what was being done for his Mom. He left town having only added to the problem. Sometimes it is the son that lives in the city with his Mom. He might have a demanding job that involves traveling a couple of weeks in the month.

In being realistic, everyone should be prepared financially for prospect of paying for services required once someone becomes unable to care for themselves due a chronic debilitating illness. Relying entirely on family members is rarely a good solution. Having insurance protection preserves choices about where and how services are received, and benefits the immediate and extended family members who are concerned about your well-being. This is the type of insurance that you hope will not be needed, BUT should you need long-term health care services having the necessary financial resources will make a significant difference.

A married couple accumulates assets and resources to be used during retirement years. All too often, if one of them has an extended health care need, financial resources are depleted. This makes it difficult for the surviving spouse to have the financial resources should they also have the need for services for themselves in the future. Thus it is imperative that you be conscientious in preserving as much money as possible while doing everything you can for your loved one needing personal and medical services now. Insurance that covers a chronic illness helps preserve those resources for the surviving spouse.

If you are single, consider siblings or other family members who might be affected if you need long-term health care services. They would be very concerned about your well-being, especially if you had limited choices related to your care.

Unfortunately, this type of insurance has historically been marketed as a product for retirees; there are no age restrictions on who may need long-term health care. Many of you reading this book may be caring for an adult child because of an accident or depilating illness requiring long–term care.

One classic example was the unexpected injury Christopher Reeves, 'Superman', suffered in a horseback riding accident. Mr. Reeves was 43 years old when he had an accident that left him paralyzed for ten years before his death. His loving wife, Dana, cared for him until his death. Unfortunately, she was diagnosed with lung cancer and died less than a year after her husband's death. Most would agree that the years of care-giving compromised her health.

A common misconception among the general public is that health insurance pays for the type of long-term health care that Christopher Reeves required. Remember, health insurance pays ONLY for the physician, hospital, medications, and other services related to a short-term accident or illness. Once care becomes custodial in nature it is NOT covered by health insurance. Long-term care insurance provides the financial resources to pay the professionals to take care of daily needs such as bathing, dressing, feeding; thus, relieving much of the physical strain on the family. The family can then concentrate on giving love and emotional support to the one needing care.

Fortunately, today we have options that were not available to our parents. They were often *forced* to choose a nursing home when they became unable to care for themselves independently. Professional services for home health care were almost nonexistent. Demographics were also different. Families lived in closer proximity to each other, and the "man of the house" worked and provided the total income for the family while the woman stayed home to care for the family. Additionally, there were fewer two income families, which facilitated care giving for the sick or elderly within the family unit. You may remember this situation portrayed in the television show, 'The Waltons.'

Today, two- income families are by far the majority, followed by single parents. These family units have been dubbed the "sandwich generation" because they are responsible for school age kids and aging parents. Quitting an income-producing job is often not an option when care for a parent becomes necessary. Having professionals providing care-giving services to a parent can make it easier on the whole family.

High Quality Care

Long-term care insurance is important because it will allow me to pass on my estate to my children rather than deplete it thought long-term care expenses. I purchased the insurance because I wanted to have high quality care when needed without worrying about the drain on finances. I am now a caregiver for my wife, and the insurance I purchased has helped tremendously through the benefits provided. It has allowed me to have peace of mind in providing quality care and in knowing that it will continue. I liked working with Babs because she is a knowledgeable professional who stays abreast of the regulations and researches the product to provide the most 'bang for the buck."

~John

Notes & Questions:

CHAPTER 3

QUESTION 2: WHAT CRITERION SHOULD I USE TO EVALUATE THE COMPANY THAT IS SELLING LONG-TERM CARE INSURANCE?

A company's ratings are important in the selection of any insurance product. For long-term care additional criterion should be evaluated because this is such a new product. You want to know if the company you are considering for your long-term care insurance has demonstrated a commitment to the long-term care market. Some companies began selling this product and then decided that it was not a profitable market for them. As a rule of thumb, when an insurance company introduces a new product, it takes approximately 15 years for that company to determine profitability. We have seen large, reputable companies get in the long-term care insurance market, stay a few years and then decide to get out of the long-term care insurance market as they had not properly priced the product and were facing millions of dollars in losses due to the increasing costs of care. In some cases, the policy holders have seen significant increases in their premiums, but other cases the rates have not been affected due to the company choosing to stop offering the product. I personally own a long-term care policy that I purchased 20 years ago. The company no longer sells long-term care and I have not seen any changes to the service I have received and have had only a minimum increase in the premiums I pay.

It is recommended that you buy long-term care from an insurance company that has been selling long-term care for a minimum of 10 years and are selling their product in every state. Buy from a large national company that has a variety of insurance products such as long-term care insurance, life insurance, annuities, mutual funds, 401k plans, etc. Long-term care is just *a part* of a comprehensive portfolio. You can find out about an insurance company's ratings by calling one or more of the independent rating services listed below. AM Best is probably the most well-known rating service. Be certain that you buy your long-term care insurance from a company that has 'A' or better from AM Best. Their phone number is 908-439-2200. Other rating services are Standard and Poor's (212-438-7280), Moody's (212-553-1658), and Fitch (800-853-4842).

State Insurance Departments can offer information on the claims and complaint history of insurance companies.

Notes & Questions:

_____

_____

_____

_____

_____

_____

_____

_____

_____

_____

_____

_____

_____

_____

_____

_____

_____

_____

_____

_____

_____

_____

CHAPTER 4

QUESTION 3: WHAT TYPES OF LONG-TERM CARE POLICIES ARE AVAILABLE?

WHEN YOU PURCHASE long-term care insurance look carefully at how the benefits will be paid once you become eligible to receive them. You are buying long-term care insurance for a future time when you may need professional services because you are unable to care for yourself independently. Some contracts deliver the benefit by the indemnity method while others deliver the benefit by the reimbursement method.

The **indemnity method** pays your full daily benefit amount every day a covered service is received, regardless of the cost of that service. For example, if your plan has a $300 per day benefit at the time you become eligible for benefits, and you receive services from a licensed professional costing $200 for that day, you will still receive a check for $300 for that day. That extra $100 in excess of the charges will be very useful for other expenses associated with long-term health care such as prescription medications, medical equipment, and specialized transportation. You can also put the excess money in your bank account for future needs.

The **reimbursement method**, as the name suggests, reimburses the care provider or the insured up to the actual expenses. For example, if your plan has a $300 per day benefit, and you receive services from a licensed professional costing $200 per day, you will be reimbursed $200 for actual expenses. The $100 difference will remain in the plan, thus extending the length of the benefit period.

Reimbursement can be on a daily or monthly basis; always select the <u>monthly</u> reimbursement. Whatever services are required over a period of a month will be reimbursed up to your monthly benefit amount. Some days the services needed may be more than your daily benefit amount, or some days it may be less. By selecting the monthly reimbursement plan, you have fewer out-of-pocket expenses to pay.

Any plan you consider should pay for benefits at all levels of care and in any setting, such as, home care, adult day care, assisted-living and nursing home. The plan should also include coverage for both skilled and non-skilled care. Approximately 80% of long-term care is received outside of a nursing home, either at home or in an assisted living facility. Most plans offer a choice of 100%, 75% or 50% of the nursing home benefit for home and/or community care which includes assisted living and adult day care. Unless the premium is the main consideration in purchasing a plan, I recommend that you choose the same benefit amount for services at home as you choose for a nursing facility. Most long-term care is received at home, so the home care benefit is extremely important to a well-designed plan. If you want to remain at home even when you need round-the-clock care, make sure you clearly communicate this with your insurance agent. Your plan can be designed with a daily benefit that is *at least* 30% more than a plan that assumes five to eight hours of services at home.

Many group plans offered through employers only offer 50% of the nursing home benefit to be available for home care. If you are thinking about purchasing a plan through your employer, inquire about the home care benefit and then purchase the policy on the basis of receiving an adequate home care benefit.

The importance of inflation protection cannot be overstated. Carefully consider the impact of inflation in the cost of services when purchasing a long-term care insurance plan. What would protect you today will have little value to you 20 years from now with the rising cost of healthcare services. I expect to see retirement and lifestyle options available to future retirees that aren't available today, partly because the 'baby boomer' generation will demand better services and better facilities. Naturally, the best options will most likely be the most expensive.

Your plan should provide resources that allow you to take advantage of all the options available if and when you need long-term care. When I talk to my clients I always *stress* that they are buying a future benefit. I encourage them to focus on the future benefit rather than on the current benefit printed on the proposal. By doing a projection of the benefit that will be available to them in 20 or 30 years down the road, it becomes easier to visualize how a long-term care insurance plan fits into the overall financial plan.

Notes & Questions:

_____

_____

_____

_____

_____

_____

_____

_____

_____

_____

_____

_____

_____

_____

_____

_____

_____

_____

_____

_____

CHAPTER 5

QUESTION 4: AT WHAT AGE SHOULD YOU BUY LONG-TERM CARE INSURANCE?

IN ORDER TO answer this question we should look at *reasons* for buying long-term care insurance at different ages.

Ages 50 to 60

It is best to begin investigating long-term care insurance in your early 50's since the premiums are driven by age and current health. Additionally, there is something about age 50 that catapults our thinking from the life we have had to the life that lies before us. (Maybe it is because we get our first mailing from AARP!) Retirement seems to take on a greater meaning, and articles about retirement suddenly catch our attention.

If you plan to retire at age 65, you have 15 years to be prepared for those all-important years when you are living on the planning that you have previously done. At age 50, you still time to make a difference in what that picture will look like. If you are like most people, you are amazed that you have already lived a half a century and you can't fathom how the time has passed quickly. You may still be helping your kids become adults or financing their journey. You may also begin to realize that your parents are getting older. If you haven't purchased long-term care insurance by this time, start doing your homework. The premiums will never be lower and, if you are in good health, you will qualify for the coverage and possibly get a discount because of your health history.

Another reason to consider buying long-term care at age 50 is the availability of an accelerated payment option. This is an excellent method of payment if it fits into your budget. For example, If you are 50, you can elect to own a 'paid up' plan in 10 years, by age 60. When buying the 'paid up' plans you are buying the type of insurance that is a combination of life insurance that includes a 'chronic illness' rider. You will be paying all of your premiums during your earning years in order to own a 'paid up' plan during your retirement years. Premiums for this type of plan are considerably higher, but owning a 'paid up' plan at retirement makes this option almost too attractive to pass up.

For those of you who have disability insurance through the workplace, please remember that the disability that you own typically expires at age 65 or 67. As you get closer to the time the disability coverage expires, your potential benefit due to a claim will be less because the benefit will be paying out for fewer years. For example, if you are 50 years old and become disabled, your policy will pay benefits for 15 to 17 years, depending on the terms of the contract. If, on the other hand, you become disabled when you are 60 years old, your benefits will be payable for 5 to 7 years. A long-term care insurance policy with inflation protection will have increasing benefits. Every year you own the policy, the benefits payable during a claim increase.

Premiums for an individual disability policy can be substantial, and the total amount payable to you decreases every year you own the policy. Evaluate your policy to determine what the policy's value is to your current financial plan.

To illustrate my point, I will share an experience. I was recently working with a 55-year-old, successful business owner who had an individual disability policy with a monthly premium of approximately $250. His business had developed a plan, that if he should become disabled, the income from the business would continue to support his family making his disability policy less valuable to him. I suggested that he take the premiums he was paying for his disability policy and buy a long-term care insurance policy for himself and his wife. Both of them were young and healthy, they were able to purchase an excellent comprehensive plan that included inflation protection with the same premium dollars.

If you are an employee of a company and your family is dependent on your paycheck, it is important to keep your disability coverage during earning years.

In some situations, I like to stack a long-term care policy on top of current disability coverage. This gives the family extra protection in the event of a catastrophic injury or illness. The disability benefit typically replaces 60% of one's earnings. If the employer provides the benefit, it will be taxable and thus create a considerable shortfall for the family. Long-term care insurance can help to make up that difference and pay for the health care services that may be needed down the road. When the disability expires, the long-term care will continue to pay out benefits for as long as the contract stipulates.

Before buying long-term care insurance in place of disability insurance, one must understand what triggers the benefit in each policy. Disability insurance is triggered by being unable to do 'the material and substantial duties of your occupation'. Long-term care insurance is triggered if you are unable to perform certain 'activities of daily living' or have a cognitive impairment such as Alzheimer's or dementia. It is entirely possible that one would qualify for disability benefits and not qualify for long-term care insurance.

So, if you don't already own long-term care insurance, now is the time to evaluate this insurance plan as it relates to your particular retirement needs. Premiums increase significantly as you get older, and health issues may prevent you from qualifying for a long-term care plan.

Ages 18 to 30

Why buy long-term care insurance at age 18? Most 18-year-olds are still being financed in varying degrees by their parents, and a disability at such a young age would be devastating and could last a lifetime. Health insurance pays the doctor and the hospital in the event of an accident or illness, but once the disability or illness becomes custodial in nature, health insurance no longer pays benefits. It is important to understand that a long- term care event could happen at any age and health insurance may not be enough. At these ages, it might be wise to consider owning a life insurance contract that includes a provision for a catastrophic health event and will pay out some or all of the death in the event of a health care crisis.

Age 30 to 50

If you are in a profession that provides disability insurance for you, or you own an individual disability policy consider owning long-term care insurance as an add-on to your disability coverage. Physicians and other high-end professions, for example, are limited in the amount of disability coverage they can own which leaves a sizeable gap between their disability benefit and their earnings. If you do not have other resources to fill the gap, it would be wise for you to purchase a life contract that includes a rider for a chronic illness or catastrophic health care event.

A long-term care policy is another option if you do not own disability insurance, either because it isn't available to you, or because it is too expensive. A policy will provide some financial protection against a life-changing catastrophic event. If you don't own disability insurance because it is not available to you or it is too expensive, investigate a long-term care policy which will provide some financial protection against a life-changing, catastrophic event. Remember, having a long-term health care need is a huge issue without having a financial and emotional crisis to deal with as well.

Recently, I was working with a computer technician in his mid-40's. He was concerned about the financial well-being of his family if he became disabled. When we looked at a disability policy, we found that the premiums were very high and the benefits offered for the premiums were insufficient. Since the client felt he could perform most of his professional duties from home, we decided to look at a long-term care insurance policy instead. As a result he will receive twice the benefits he would have received from a disability contract for half the premium He is comfortable with the concept of long-term care insurance providing a safety net to meet a loss of income due to an accident or illness.

Age 60 to 70

Fortunately, a well-designed long-term care plan is still considered a bargain compared to the cost of services due to a long-term health care need. Look at all the options of a plan design. If you are still working but plan to retire at 65, you will continue to pay the premiums after you retire. Make sure you buy a plan that fits your post retirement budget, because buying a policy and then letting it go is a senseless waste of money. Consider using a 3% compound inflation rider rather than a 5% compound inflation rider so your premium fits your budget.

Ages 70 to 80

Even at this age, it may still wise to consider buying long-term care insurance, especially if you are 75 or younger.

Early in the evolution of long-term care when the product first came on the market, many of the people that were inquiring about it were over age 70. Most purchased the coverage as protection for their families and their assets. Now, more than 5 million Americans are living with Alzheimer's disease (nearly one in two people over 85), and it is forecasted that 16 million people will be living with Alzheimer's disease by 2050. Long-term care coverage is especially important for families who care for someone with Alzheimer's disease. The care giving in this situation is exhausting and help from outside sources is almost essential to the well-being of the caregiver.

My Mom had dementia in her late 80's that continued and became progressively worse over 4 years. We were fortunate to have a housekeeper with a nursing background to stay with Mom so my father could go about his daily routine. In the evenings, Dad took care of Mom, but it wasn't easy. As a family which included a brother and sister and spouses, we, often talked about when it might be time to move Mom to a nursing home. It was then that I really understood how very difficult that decision is to make. When I would think about my Mom being in a place unfamiliar to her and not knowing if all her needs were being attended to as she was accustomed to, it was more than I or my siblings wanted to bear. Nor did we want Dad to then be at home alone after all these many years with our Mom. Before that became the only alternative for Mom, she passed away. Dad has now lived another 4 years and is a spry 96 year old who still drives and goes to the office. I think Dad is doing so well because we had help with Mom and it wasn't entirely on his shoulders to be her caregiver. He spent his time with her being loving and encouraging and a paid caregiver helped Mom with the difficult duties of bathing and dressing and feeding on a daily basis.

Age 80 and above

This age group should investigate the alternatives to individual long-term care insurance. An annuities or life insurance with a long-term care rider would be a good choice. See the information on LINKED BENEFITS for additional information.

Planning Ahead for the Golden Years:

Having gone through in-home care, plus two hospital stays and now seven months of costly nursing home care for my 90-year old mother, my husband and I saw the need to buy our own long-term care insurance policy. We want to be financially secure during our golden years at a price we can afford now. Plus, this will give us more peace of mind in the future.

~ Joyce Rye Kasberg

Notes & Questions:

_____

_____

_____

_____

_____

_____

_____

_____

_____

_____

_____

_____

_____

_____

_____

_____

_____

_____

_____

_____

_____

_____

_____

CHAPTER 6

QUESTION 5: ARE THERE ANY TAX ADVANTAGES FOR PURCHASING LONG-TERM CARE INSURANCE?

The Federal Government sent a strong message to Americans in 1996 with the passage of the Health Insurance Portability and Accountability Act (HIPAA) and in 2006 with the passage of the Pension Protection Act. The Health Insurance Portability and Accountability Act (HIPAA) created "qualified long-term care insurance." If a policy meets the requirements specified in the Act, it receives significant tax advantages. This Act also gives tax incentives to buyers of long-term care insurance.

The federal government has legitimate concerns about the ability of Medicare and Medicaid to provide for the long-term needs of the baby boomer generation. It is estimated that the number of people needing long-term care services exceeds nine million per year and will increase to over 12 million by 2020. Our government recognizes the potential for a healthcare crisis and is encouraging people to purchase long-term care insurance by offering financial incentives.

The most significant tax advantage is for business owners. Businesses that are organized as a LLC, a Subchapter S, or a Partnership can deduct long-term care premiums for the business owner and a spouse (whether the spouse is working in the business or not) up to a certain limit determined by the owner's and spouse's age. A business that is organized as a C Corporation can take a full deduction of the premiums regardless of age. Employer payments for long-term care group premiums are also tax deductible to the employer. When the benefits are received, they are tax free up to the limits set by the government. In 2015 up to $330 per day of benefits paid from a long-term care insurance policy is tax free, and this applies to individuals as well as business owners.

Each year the federal government has increased the amount that can be received as tax-free income. This is one part of the tax code that allows you to receive a tax deduction for premiums paid as well as a tax-free benefit at claim time. With all the tax incentives being offered by the federal government, it is encouraging to know that people are looking ahead and purchasing long-term care insurance rather than relying on Medicare or Medicaid as a funding source for long-term care needs.

Individual Taxpayers

Premiums paid by individuals who are buying long-term care insurance (who are not business owners) are deductible as medical expenses for itemized deduction purposes, and the amount that can be deducted is determined by one's age-bracket. Long-term care insurance is treated as accident and health insurance (IRC 7702B(2)(1) The deduction is limited to the lesser of actual premium paid or eligible premium amounts. IRC 213(d)(1)(D), 213(d)(10)

In 2015 the eligible premium per person:	
Age 40 or less	$380
Age 41-50	$710
Age 51-60	$1430
Age 61-70	$3,800
Age 71 and older	$4,750

Medical expense deduction is allowable to extent that such expenses (including payment of the eligible premium) exceed 10% of the AGI (Adjusted Gross Income) IRC 213(d) (10)

If you do not itemize deductions, then you cannot take a deduction for long-term care premiums.

For a MSA (Medical saving Account) and a HSA (Health savings Account) eligible premium is considered a qualified

For the employee:

- Deductible by the employee who itemizes (subject to the limitations above).

- May NOT be paid through a cafeteria plan IRC 125(1)

- May NOT be paid through an FSA or similar arrangement IRC 106(c)

Premium paid by employer:

- Employer provided long-term care insurance is treated as an accident and health plan IRC 7702B)a)(3)

- Deductible by the employer (subject to reasonable compensation)

- Total (not eligible) premium paid is excluded from employee's income IRC 106(a)

C-Corporation

- Treated as 'employee'. See above.

Sole-Proprietor

- Eligible for Self-Employed health insurance deduction, which is taken 'above the line' Line 29 of IRS form 1040 IRC 162(i)

S-Corporation (greater than 2% shareholder with W-2)

- Limited to lesser of actual premium paid or eligible premium IRC 213(d)(10)

Partnership (any %)

- Eligible premium in current year

Limited Liability Corporation (LLC)

- Depends on how the entity files

The deduction for business set up as Sole-Proprietor, S-corporation, Partnership and Limited Liability Corporation are NOT limited to 10% of AGI threshold as outlined above.

When benefits are received they are NOT included in income. IRC 104(a)(3) 770B(a)(2)

Please note that the information given with respect to this summary is not to be interpreted as specific legal or tax advice. The Corporation for Long-Term Care Certification, Inc. provides the content of this summary, and neither their employees nor representatives are authorized to give legal or tax advice. You are encouraged to get advice on legal and tax matters from those who are authorized in those matters.

Some contracts have Non-forfeiture benefits (return of premium):

- Available only upon total surrender or death

- May not be borrowed or pledged

- Included in gross income to extent of any deduction or exclusion allowed with respect to premium   IRC 770B(b)(2)(C)

I am often asked if I think the government will take away these tax incentives. On the contrary, I believe we should expect them to be expanded. I hope to see an above-the-line tax deduction and the inclusion of long-term care insurance in 'cafeteria plans'. The current Medicaid system will go broke sooner than later if serious attention is not directed toward encouraging the private sector to purchase long-term care insurance protection, thereby spreading the risk with the insurance industry rather than with the government.

Check with your tax advisor or your accountant for specific advice related to your situation.

Notes & Questions:

CHAPTER 7

QUESTION 6: WHAT PARAMETERS SHOULD I USE TO DETERMINE IF I SHOULD BUY LONG-TERM CARE INSURANCE OR PAY FOR SERVICES WITH MY ACCUMULTED ASSETS?

When first edition of this book was printed in the spring of 2008, who could have imagined that the economy would see such a drastic decline? Many people who were comfortable paying long-term healthcare costs out of pocket have seen their portfolios shrink by 40% or more. Most believe the country will hit the elusive bottom and then begin its climb, thus regaining some of its losses. But what if you had decided to 'self-insure' and needed to pay long-term health care cost during a downturn in the market? Selling stocks to fund your long-term health care needs would further devastate your financial picture that had taken years to create. The benefits provided by long-term care insurance are not subject to market swings, so owning long-term care insurance should serve as the risk management component of a well-designed portfolio, preventing you from being forced to sell stocks and assets when it is not to your advantage.

So ask yourself, "Can I comfortably assume the financial risk of long-term health care now or at the time I am most likely to need long-term care?" According to a recent statistic, 69% of those over 65 will need long-term healthcare at some point in their lives. Prudence dictates that you should consider yourself in that 69% group. Assume that you will need to pay for long-term health care services at some time, and then decide what source of funds you will use to pay for those services. Do you have stocks you can liquidate? Do you have other assets that you are willing to liquidate and use? If the answer is yes, then buying long-term care insurance is not essential.

The potential need for long-term healthcare is a matter of significant financial risk. Long-term care planning should be a part of a well-designed financial plan that assesses your current situation and future assets and income. Be certain that you have considered that cost of services today are expected to rise dramatically within the next 20 years and perhaps even triple what they are today. Be prepared to either pay for the services of long-term healthcare out of pocket or to transfer that risk to the insurance company, provided you qualify for coverage.

Stewart Welch III, founder of the Welch Group, a wealth management firm in Birmingham, Alabama, and author of several books including **The Idiot's Guide to Getting Rich** said, "I used to advise our clients who had a net worth exceeding $2 million to 'self-insure'. But what I have found is that people, particularly people of wealth, are adamant that they remain in their homes rather than enter a nursing home facility. The result is often twenty-four hour nursing care, seven days a week and the resulting costs are astronomical. In one recent case, both the husband and wife required round-the-clock professional care by two separate teams costing over $200,000 a year!" That is in today's dollars. Remember due to inflation, those costs will be significantly higher 20 years from now.

I have many clients who are wealthy and yet have purchased long-term care insurance. Premiums are insignificant when measured against the true cost of long-term healthcare, which is a combination of the actual cost of long-term care services and the opportunity cost of that expenditure. Dismantling a financial portfolio is stressful and a quick sale of assets is usually to the buyer's advantage, not the seller's. Wealthy individuals calculate the loss of investment earnings and carefully consider that being forced to sell stocks at inopportune times may be costly for them. The premium is tax deductible in many instances, giving another incentive to add this layer of protection to one's assets.

When deciding how much to spend on a long-term care policy, factor in your fixed income resources. For example, if you are receiving (or will receive) $2,000 a month from Social Security, buy a monthly long-term care benefit that coordinates with your Social Security benefits. If the cost of nursing home in your area is $8,000, buy a plan that pays a benefit of $7,000 a month and use half of your Social Security benefit to make up the difference. This also applies to pension benefits. The offset will reduce the premium without adding to the risk. This strategy will not work if an inflation rider is not included in your long-term care policy so that the benefits keep up with the rising costs of health care services.

If you have VA benefits and thereby are likely to qualify for long-term care through the VA, I recommend that you buy only a two year plan. This gives you services at home before you qualify for the VA (it can take time to be admitted to a VA hospital).

> *I am a small business owner and a Viet Nam era veteran. I have made plans to spend my last few years at the VA facility but I still need the security of long-term care. This will take care of many of the expenses of unknown origins that I know will occur. This also gives me the added knowledge that my business will have time to recover with my absence.*
>
> ## David Crawford, Business Owner

On the other end of the spectrum ask yourself, "If I have limited assets, should I buy long-term care insurance?" If you can pay the premiums on a minimum plan *without* placing a burden on your lifestyle, consider an assisted-living and facility plan with a two or three-year benefit. Plans of this type don't cover home care, but they do cover assisted-living facilities.

We are fortunate to have a government program to serve those in the community who cannot afford to pay for nursing home services; however, by qualifying for Medicaid, you give up choices on where you want to receive care. If you are married, you put your spouse at risk of having inadequate financial resources for his or her life and lifestyle.

If you think that you might need the services provided by Medicaid, be sure to consult with an elder care attorney or an attorney that has expertise in estate planning. The rules for qualifying have changed making it much harder to qualify for the benefits. In some states, the state is holding the children that live in the state where the parent is utilizing the Medicaid benefit responsible for the charges. Of all the reasons that people give for buying long-term insurance, not being a burden on their children is mentioned most often. This goes back to an earlier chapter; children are caught in the 'sandwich generation', trying to raise a family and care for elderly parents and maintain a career. This is partly due to people living longer and partly due couples are starting their own families later in their marriage or getting married in their 30s rather than in their early 20s. Also, we are primarily a dual income society and both incomes are necessary for the lifestyle of the family.

Notes & Questions:

CHAPTER 8

QUESTION 7: WHICH INFLATION PROTECTION SHOULD BE ADDED TO THE POLICY SO THE PLAN KEEPS UP WITH THE RISING COSTS OF LONG-TERM CARE SERVICES?

A number of options are available to help your long-term care plan keep up with the rising cost of care.

Future Purchase Offer: This product is designed to protect the insured for 15 to 20 years, and inflation protection is not built into this plan. Every three years, however, the insured is given the opportunity to increase the policy's benefits regardless of changes in health. The increase in policy benefits would also have a corresponding increase in premium. My concern is that the initially low premiums would increase so dramatically that the insured would rather settle for a much lower benefit than pay the ever-increasing premiums. Consequently, at the time long-term healthcare services are needed the benefit is inadequate to meet the needs of the insured. However, that some benefit is certainly better than none.

5% Simple Inflation Protection: By adding this rider, the original benefit amount will increase by 5% each year, and in 20 years the original benefit will have doubled. In many cases, this is the option I recommend, particularly for those 70 years old and older. I also use simple inflation for people in their 50s and 60s if they have considerable assets that can contribute to a long-term care need. The simple inflation option costs less than the compound inflation option; however you'll gain more coverage each year with compound inflation protection. Carefully consider the simple inflation option so you will have adequate benefits when care is needed.

5% Compound Inflation Protection: The original benefit will increase by 5% of the previous years' benefit and in effect will double in approximately fifteen years. The power of compounding is almost magical and will far outpace simple inflation in approximately 30 years. Again, a careful analysis of one's circumstances is necessary to determine which inflation option to add to the plan. Sometimes the choice is easy. For example, compound inflation makes sense for people in their 30's and 40's. I advise clients to start with a lower benefit amount knowing that the benefit will inflate to appropriate amounts during retirement years. The compound inflation rider costs more than the simple inflation rider for obvious reasons. The financial obligation of the insurance carrier is much greater in the latter years of the contract, and with people living longer the projected pay out amount is much greater. With the current state of the economy, I expect that many carriers will reconsider the option of compound inflation because they are going to have difficulty investing the premiums collected and get a return that allows them to pay the claims and make a profit. Some carriers are already redesigning their long-term care insurance plans and pricing the compound inflation rider considerably higher than their previous plans.

3% Compound: Many carriers are offering a 3% compound inflation rider at competitive prices to drive the market to select this inflation rider over the 5% compound rider. Using this rider the benefit doubles in approximately 24 years for the time of purchase.

No inflation: If you are 65 years of age or older, consider a long-term care insurance plan   consider a long-term care insurance plan that is one and a half to two times the current cost of care without an added inflation rider. You can determine which plan is the best option by making a comparison between a plan that has a higher benefit amount without inflation and a plan that has a lower benefit option with simple inflation. Consider your current health as well as your family health history in making a decision. Many 75 year olds will live into their nineties; a good plan design will take longevity into account.

See the chart at the back of the book to compare simple and compound rates at 3% and 5%.

> *"No one looks forward to a time when he or she is dependent on others for personal physical care. Long-term care insurance ensures a sense of dignity, control and self-reliance during a time in one's life that can otherwise feel very out of control. Having a ready source of funds to pay for the related costs make all the difference. LTC insurance does not eliminate the fear, pain, heartache, or anxiety associated with physical or mental decline, but it does provide peace of mind that cannot be measured monetarily."*
>
> ~ Jan L. Brakefield, M.S., C.F.P.,
> Assistant Professor,
> Department of Consumer Sciences,
> The University of Alabama

Notes & Questions:

CHAPTER 9

QUESTION 8: WHAT BENEFIT PERIOD SHOULD I BUY?

Long-term care insurance is paid over different periods. When you purchase a long-term care policy, you will be able to select the benefit period. The most common ones are 2 years, 3 years, 4 years, 5 years and 6 years. Defining the benefit in terms of years is confusing; the benefits in the policy will last the specified number of years IF you use the maximum amount of benefit dollars every month. In most incidents when care is being received at home, services are not used every day. On the days when services are not used the benefit dollars stay in the plan. A three year plan could stay in force for 4 years if services are not exhausted to the maximum amount every day or month depending on how the plan is designed.

Insurance carriers offered lifetime benefits when the plans and policies were first designed. By 2008 insurance carriers that were still in the long-term care market were removing the lifetime benefits from their contracts and selling to the public new plans that had limited benefit periods. These carriers stopped assuming the risk of possibly paying benefits for 15 years because a policyholder diagnosed with Alzheimer's disease at age 60, and other than the cognitive impairment was healthy. A good example is President Ronald Reagan; had he owned a lifetime plan when he was diagnosed with Alzheimer's disease, his plan would have paid benefits over the remaining 11 years of his life.

In most cases, claims are paid out over much shorter periods than lifetime. Claims are usually paid for only 3 to 4 years. Why is this? For someone to qualify for the long-term care benefits, he or she must be unable to perform normal activities of daily living such as bathing, dressing and eating, or have a sever cognitive impairment such as Alzheimer's disease or dementia. When a person's health reaches the point of needing this type of assistance, statistically he or she will live only 3 or 4 years longer.

When I discuss long-term care insurance with someone, I explain long-term care insurance as a right-brain/left-brain decision. The right brain is analytical and values statistics when deciding how much risk to assume and how much money to spend. The concept of a person's 'risk tolerance' comes into play. The left-brain decision is based on emotions and recognizes that owning long-term care insurance is a matter of peace of mind, security and dignity of life.

One of the most important reasons people buy long-term care insurance is for peace of mind; therefore it is very important to assume a premium that you can comfortably pay until the benefit is needed. Don't spend so much on long-term care insurance that you lose sleep every time you write a check to pay the premium. Remember, unless you choose an accelerated-payment option (paying the plan over a shorter period of time), you will pay the premiums until the benefit is needed or until your death.

Personal experience can dictate what type of plan you choose. If, for example, you have a family member who needs long-term healthcare for an extended period of time (i.e. 10 to 15 years), you may ignore the statistics and buy the longest benefit period available.

I like to think of long-term care insurance as a safety net to protect the insured from unexpected costs of long-term healthcare. The policy should fit with other components of your financial plan so the premiums are reasonable for your particular financial situation. If other resources such as retirement benefits, inheritances and social security benefits can be utilized to pay for long-term care services, a good long-term care insurance plan should reflect those resources.

Long-term care insurance preserves choices, so the determining factors should be quality and location of care received. Since most people choose to remain in their homes or in a retirement community, the plan you select should reflect the costs associated with either of these choices. If you desire to remain in your home and have round-the-clock care, you should purchase a plan with a generous daily benefit appropriate to the cost of services in your area.

In choosing a benefit period, you should get a good understanding of what the benefit will be at the time you will need it. For example, if a 60 year old man buys a long-term care plan that has a 5 year benefit period and an initial benefit amount of $50,000 a year with a 5% simple inflation rider, he will have a safety net of $250,000 in tax free benefit dollars. At the age of 80, his safety net will have grown to $500,000.

When you purchase a long-term care plan, you purchase a future benefit. Although you own the benefits the day you approved and pay your first premium, it's important to know exactly what long-term care benefit you will own (because of the inflation protection) in your eighties and nineties to help you determine the amount of coverage to buy. For instance, if your future long-term care insurance benefit is over $700,000 at age 85 *and* you have appropriate protection for your other assets *and* the premiums are right for your budget, then this is the plan to buy.

Several factors should be considered when choosing a benefit period. One important consideration is the difference between life expectancies of men and women. When talking to a married couple I like to say, "Long-term care insurance is coverage that men buy for their wives. The wife is usually around when her husband needs long-term care services and she brings him turkey sandwiches while he sits in the recliner and manages the TV remote control. He then dies, goes to glory, and she lives 10 or more years facing the very real prospect of needing long-term care services without the assistance of her spouse".

Married men are more likely to receive services at home and spend less time in a nursing home. Women typically outlive their husbands 7 out of 10 times and may be unable to stay at home without oversight and a measure of safety provided by a spouse. Additionally, women may need nursing home care for longer periods of time. (You may have noticed the low ratio of men to women in nursing homes). So, when considering benefit periods, consider these differences and purchase a plan that gives the wife the benefit she may need.

If you are single and buying long-term care insurance, understand that you may not be able to stay safely in your own home alone. You may need to be in a retirement community or in an assisted living facility, so buy a plan that coordinates with the cost of those living arrangements. Before buying long-term care insurance make some calls to the assisted living facilities and retirement communities in your area and inquire about the cost of being a resident before you need services and the cost of services should you need them.

Forty five percent of all long-term health care claims are paid out to those under age 65. When a young person needs long-term health care due to an accident or a debilitating illness, he or she is more likely to recover and go on to lead a productive life. Then at some point in life, he or she may need may need long-term care services again. When purchasing long-term care insurance for someone younger than fifty, consider a **'restoration of benefits'** rider for the plan. See the Glossary of terms for an explanation of this rider.

Notes & Questions:

_____

_____

_____

_____

_____

_____

_____

_____

_____

_____

_____

_____

_____

_____

_____

_____

_____

_____

_____

_____

_____

_____

CHAPTER 10

QUESTION 9: WHAT ARE LINKED BENEFITS?

Leverage Your Assets

Even with Medicare, the greatest potential threat to your retirement planning is an extended health care need: few people have planned for spending $80,000 to $100,000 a year for services related to a chronic illness or other health issues common to old age. (This is in the south; the cost can be much greater in other parts of the country). To address this need for additional financial resources, the insurance industry introduced long-term health care insurance in the early 90s as has been discussed in the earlier chapters. All went well for about 20 years, until the companies offering the insurance realized that they had not properly priced their products to meet the demands at claim time and so began a series of rate increases. Meanwhile, other companies decided to discontinue even offering the product. This 'upheaval' sent many insurance carriers back to the drawing board; the problem was not going away, there needed to be a better solution. The solution has come in the form of 'linked products'. We now have combination products, life insurance and annuities with riders that allow the person access to 'living benefits'; meaning, you do not have to die to collect.

> The tax laws allow a tax-free death benefit and long-term care benefits that are income tax- free. These contracts have a death benefit and a 'living' benefit.

Traditional long-term care insurance is not the perfect fit for everyone. Sometimes it makes sense to use 'linked benefits'. A linked benefit might be a combination of a life insurance policy and long-term care insurance or a combination of an annuity and long-term care insurance. If it is a life insurance combination and the insured never needs long-term health care the death benefit pays out just as a typical life insurance policy. Linked benefits are a way to leverage the assets you have so that they are working much harder and smarter on your behalf. If you own a life insurance policy that has cash value and are insurable, it might be wise to move the cash value from the policy you own into a linked benefit policy that would allow you to own long-term care protection and life insurance. A word of caution, if you need the long-term care benefits you will be exhausting the death benefit dollars. At your death your family will not have the benefit of a lump sum death benefit payment to help with the needs of a surviving spouse or outstanding debt or funeral expenses. In other words, if the death benefit is critical to the surviving spouse, family, or needed for estate tax purposes it would be advisable to own long-term care insurance separate from your life insurance policy.

This type of policy is particularly attractive to those who are comfortable paying for long-term care out of their pocket, but see the advantages to leveraging the assets that they have. If you have money that you do not anticipate needing, making that money do some 'double duty' might be wise for all concerned. Even if you are comfortable about having the assets to 'self-insure', writing a $100,000 check for long-term care for just one year of care and the prospect of writing that check for five or more years is probably not what you would want to do, given the much better option of the insurance company paying for your care and your assets remaining intact for investment opportunities, charities, or as part of a wealth transfer plan. If you have $50,000 or more in a safe investment it is probably not earning a very high rate of return. Would it be smarter to use that resource as a single premium on a life insurance policy that can also be used for long-term care? In many cases, the answer is yes.

Some companies that offer linked benefits will guarantee a return of your deposit – as long as no benefits have been paid or loans taken. If you ever change your mind about your decision you can retrieve your deposit, no questions asked; it is virtually risk free. If your deposit has grown due to the current interest stated in your policy and you surrender the policy, the funds in excess of the original deposit may be subject to a surrender charge, which is the penalty for early withdrawal. At the point when the 'surrender charge' is no longer in affect, you can withdraw the deposit plus the interest. The deposit is your cost basis and is tax-free upon withdrawal and the gain taxed as ordinary income. If, instead, you retain the policy and the benefits are paid out due to long-term health care or a chronic illness the cost basis (your deposit) and the gain are paid free of income taxes.

Additionally, with some contracts, if all of the benefits are paid out to cover extended health care needs the policy provides a 'residual death benefit' of 10% of the original death benefit for beneficiaries. For example, if the original policy has a death benefit of $300,000 and includes a long-term care rider and the entire benefit is used to provide long-term care services, the family will still receive $30,000 at the insured's death.

As with traditional long-term care there are two ways that the insurance company pays out the benefit. One method is expense reimbursement and the other is indemnity (the full monthly benefit is paid regardless of the expenses). Be sure that you are aware of how the benefit will be paid to you when you buy coverage so you will not be surprised at the time of claim. There can be advantages to either method, but I prefer getting the full benefit amount rather than having to keep up with expenses to get reimbursed.

The long-term care benefits are typically triggered by a licensed professional's certification that the insured is unable to perform normal activities of daily living like bathing, dressing, eating, transferring from one place to another without assistance or continence, or has cognitive issues such as Alzheimer's disease or dementia. Following the deductible period that is specified in the contract, the benefits of the policy are paid out at a predetermined percentage of the death benefit or as a stated monthly amount until all of the death benefit is exhausted. Some contracts will extend your benefits for long-term care even after the death benefit is exhausted for an added fee. You might say, dying too soon and living too long are *both* covered by this contract!

I like to say, "Friends don't let friends die with an annuity". Let me explain: an annuity is a good accumulation vehicle;

the money grows tax deferred and there is an opportunity for guaranteed income. Unfortunately, a majority of those owning annuities die still owning them rather than exercising the options to have them pay out as a supplement to their retirement income. The heirs of that annuity will pay, not the lesser tax of capital gain, but the higher ordinary income tax. I had a lady come to me with an annuity that her husband had purchased 30 years ago. He had paid $50,000 and it had grown to $90,000 over that period. If she had cashed it out (or left it to her son at her death), she would have paid taxes on the gain of $40,000. Because of the Pension Protection ACT of 2006, there was a solution for her; now you can move tax deferred assets into tax-free income to pay for chronic illness and extended health care, but we will get back to her situation shortly.

There are long-term care annuities available to those who are 85 or younger. One important advantage to an annuity over a stand-alone long-term care plan is the leniency of the underwriting so you more easily qualify even if there are health related issues. There are expenses inside the annuity that pay for the addition of a long-term care rider, but they are much less than those in a stand-alone policy. The account value grows tax deferred and the monthly pay out for long-term care is tied to the account value at the time of the claim. As in a stand-alone policy, access to the benefits is dependent on being unable to do two of six activities of daily living without assistance or being cognitively impaired.

The Pension Protection Act of 2006 beginning in 2010 allows for a tax free withdrawal for long-term care expenses from non-qualified annuities. In addition, annuities typically allow a tax free withdrawal annually of up to 10% of the value which can be used for other needs related to long-term care, but are not eligible to be counted as long-term care expenses, i.e., prescriptions drugs. Because of this new Act you may own an annuity that grows tax deferred and ***never*** have to pay taxes when the money is withdrawn. If you currently own an annuity you might consider exchanging it for one that has the added benefit of a long-term care rider, so should you need long-term care services, those services are available to you tax free from your annuity. . To take advantage of this strategy your annuity has to be non-qualified assets and the annuity policy has to meet the HIPPA guidelines.

Annuities offer safety and have the advantage of having funds grow tax deferred. With any annuity it is important to understand the fees associated with ownership. There are fees for the annuity itself and the additional cost for the long-term care rider. Should you not need the annuity in your lifetime, the money will pass to your heirs, and they will be responsible to pay taxes on funds received.

I recently helped a lady that owned a traditional long-term health care policy . Due to a rate increase her premiums were going to be a lot higher and at age 80 she was in very good health. If she lives 15 years and keeps the policy, she would be paying the higher premiums for a long time. She owns an annuity that had grown over the years to be about $800,000. We separated out $200,000 of the $800,000 annuity and put in to an annuity that has a long-term health care rider. The $200,000 purchased for her a long-term care benefit of $500,000. Should she need the benefits to pay for long-term care services all of the benefits will be paid out tax free; effectively taking a taxable event and turning it in to a tax free benefit. If she dies without needing the long-term care benefits, the $200,000 will pass to her son and he will be responsible to pay taxes.

In summary, linked benefits can be a win/win situation. If you do not use the benefits, the premiums paid in are not lost; the benefits are paid as a death benefit from a life insurance contract or paid to the beneficiary of an annuity contract, depending on which product you own.

NOTES & QUESTIONS:

CHAPTER 11

QUESTION 10: HOW DO I RECEIVE THE MOST FROM MY POLICY AT CLAIM TIME?

Whether you purchased your policy last year or 20 years ago, you want to receive every benefit provided through your contract at claim time.

One of my first experiences as an agent was very difficult. A couple had purchased long-term care insurance approximately two years before the wife was admitted to the hospital with an aneurism. She came home from the hospital with limited use of her right arm and leg and unable to care for herself independently. She also required assistance with activities such as bathing, dressing, and eating. The long-term care policy the couple purchased had a 90-day elimination period. I clearly remember the day that the husband called me and said, "Babs, I am exhausted and I need help." He needed relief from the constant care giving responsibilities.

Unfortunately, he had assumed that the 90-day elimination period had passed and that the benefit would now be available and begin to pay for home health services. My heart sank. In most cases, you cannot begin to satisfy the elimination period until you have received services by a qualified provider. In this case, he should have called me when his wife came home from the hospital, so we would have filed the claim at that time and made arrangements for home health services in their home in compliance with the terms of their contract. The trigger for beginning to satisfying the elimination period is receiving services from a health care provider.

Depending on the terms of the contract, just one day of services may be all that is required to receive the benefits at the end of the elimination period. My clients' particular contract stipulated that for every one day of services received, seven days could be counted toward satisfying the elimination period. In this case, he had to wait another 90 days before benefits would be payable.

When are benefits payable? Benefits are payable to policyholders who become chronically ill or disabled after the elimination period of their particular contract has been satisfied. (Most contracts require that you receive services in order to begin satisfying the elimination period.) The elimination period may be in 'service' days or on 'calendar' days. Consult the Glossary of Terms to learn the difference between 'service' days and 'calendar' days as they relate to long-term care insurance.

Some contracts have a 90 day elimination period for nursing home care, but will provide the benefits beginning the first day if care is received at home. Since most long-term care starts in the home, this is a significance difference and keeps more money in your pocket.

Benefits in a long-term care insurance contract are triggered when the insured is unable to perform normal 'activities of daily living' (ADLs) such as bathing, dressing, toileting, transferring (i.e. getting from the bed to the chair), continence and eating without substantial assistance from another person. One may also qualify for benefits if he or she but suffers from a severe cognitive impairment such as Alzheimer's disease or dementia that requires substantial supervision by another person to protect you from hurting yourself or others. The condition must be expected to last at least ninety days as determined by a licensed practitioner. Once you qualify for benefits, you should take full advantage of all the policy has to offer. For example, take advantage of the respite care benefit (see the glossary of terms) that is available each year the policy is in effect. In some contracts you can have this benefit payable during the elimination period. This benefit is designed to give the primary caregiver temporary relief from care giving duties.

Many of the contracts that I have recommended have a benefit for making changes to your home to accommodate the person needing care. This may include adding a ramp for wheelchair accessibility, additions of safety bars in the bathroom and widening the doorways. Keeping the one needing care in their own home is usually more desirable for the one needing care and usually more demanding on the caregiver.

Some long-term care insurance plans include an indemnity rider, which changes the mode of benefit payment from 'reimbursement of actual expenses' to 'payment of the full daily benefit' regardless of the expenses incurred. Take for example a 60-year-old man who is in a car accident and suffers a head injury that required daily assistance with bathing and dressing. Home care charges are $50 per day, but his daily benefit was $130 per day. For every day home care services are provided, he nets $80 for other uses related to long- term care needs. By using these services every day, he maximizes the money that is transferred from the insurance company to him. If you have a home care agency coming to your home to provide services and they come 20 days in one month, the insurance company multiplies 20 times your daily benefit and sends you a check for that amount, regardless of the actual charges for each day. Remember, the insurance company keeps what is remaining in the plan at the death of the insured with the exception of when a 'return of premium' rider is purchased.

If benefits were needed longer than the benefit period selected, it would be wise to use services on a more limited basis. In doing this, you will extend your benefit period because the money available through the plan will stay in the plan. Remember, you want the money purchased through your long-term care insurance plan to work for you. You do not want to leave it to the insurance company. If you own a plan that pays a lifetime benefit, be mindful of utilizing that benefit every day. This gives the primary caregiver the maximum relief from the arduous task of bathing and dressing, etc.

If you own a plan that reimburse for actual services received, you still have some control over how long the benefits will be payable based on how often you elect to receive the services (unless you are in a nursing home where services are continual). If your plan provides for a monthly reimbursement, the insurance company will add the charges incurred during the month and reconcile them against your monthly benefit. In some cases, you may need to pay out-of-pocket to make up for a shortfall, or you may have enough money left over to extend your benefit period.

In my experience with clients who have needed to access the benefits, the process has been to call the company providing the coverage and file a claim. The companies that I work with assign a specific person to the insured case so that there will be continuity of services provided. These 'case managers' have access the details of your contract. You are sent a claim form where you will be asked to give them the name and address of your physician. The insurance company will then get the medical records to confirm that the requirements for receiving benefits are met. The disability has to meet the requirement of needing a minimum of 90 days of recovery. This is termed "90 day certification' and is all the contracts as a requirement by the government for receiving a tax free benefit. A good example of a disability that might not meet the "90 day certification' is a knee replacement. The recovery period rarely last over two months and therefore would not qualify under the government rules.

Notes & Questions:

CHAPTER 12

WHAT IS THE PARTNERSHIP PROGRAM?

As you learn more about long-term care insurance, you may hear the word 'partnership' used. So, what is partnership in relation to long-term care and what does it mean to you?

The goal of partnership plans is for people to use the insurance company's money to pay for services before using assistance available through Medicaid. These programs were developed in the 1980s to encourage people who might be considering Medicaid as their only long-term care plan to purchase long-term care insurance instead. Partnership encourages people to purchase long-term care insurance as a way to protect their assets.

Everyone recognizes that the government should not be counted on to provide long-term healthcare services to all the elderly and disabled in our country. Medicaid was designed to help those who are truly unable to pay for long-term care. Unfortunately, under the name of 'Medicaid planning' many decided it was acceptable to take advantage of that system, designed for the poor, by finding legal ways to divest themselves of their assets in order to qualify for government assistance. This creates an additional burden to the tax payer and puts the person receiving the assistance in a position wherein they have no control over where they will receive care, and consequently, the quality of that care.

Initially, four states adopted partnership programs that allowed residents to purchase long-term care insurance policies specifically designed to meet the criterion of the partnership program, to retain a specific amount of assets and still qualify for Medicaid. Those states are California, Connecticut, Indiana and New York.

The partnership program is intended for Americans who would most likely fall into the Medicaid system. The Deficit Reduction Act of 2005 (DRA) expanded the partnership program to include all states who wanted to participate, thus providing them with much of the flexibility they had been seeking to make significant reforms to their Medicaid programs. In order to participate, each states' partnership program had to meet specific criterion including inflation protection provisions. Compound inflation protection is required for people under age 61, and some level of an inflation protection is also required for between the ages of 61 and 75.

The Deficit Reduction Act also required the Department of Health and Human Services to develop an agreement permitting those who purchased partnership plans to move between states and still use the provisions of their policy when care was needed. States can opt out, however, by not allowing not allowing the person to use the advantages of their partnership policy as it relates to qualifying for Medicaid in the new state of residence. In this case, the insured can either move back to the state where the policy was purchased or move to another state (that had not opted out) in order to qualify for the Medicaid benefits while protecting assets.

The number of states that have passed partnership legislation is expanding. Since no uniform partnership plan exits, it is important to understand the plan provided in your state. If you own a partnership plan it will generally work so that for every dollar the insurance company pays out in benefits, an equal amount of assets will be protected when qualifying for Medicaid. Some plans offer 'total asset' protection, which allows policyholders to protect all their assets from a Medicaid spend down.

The goal of partnership plans is for individuals to first use the insurance company's money to pay for services before using the assistance available through Medicaid, thus lessening the burden on Medicaid. Fortunately, the states that are offering a partnership program are requiring agents get specific training in the partnership program that is offered in their state.

If your state has a partnership program, make sure you discuss this with your agent when you inquire about long-term care insurance, especially if you think you might need government assistance along with long-term care. This would enable you to preserve some assets while still qualifying for Medicaid.

Preservation of assets for a couple could make a tremendous difference to the surviving spouse. Caregivers often suffer physically, emotionally and financially while taking care of loved ones. Long-term care insurance protects the caregiver to some degree, and the partnership program adds some financial buffer to the surviving spouse.

If Partnership programs encourage more people to own long-term care insurance as a protection for their families, then these programs will serve all of us who are tax payers. The biggest advantage is that if insurance companies pay out benefits first, this may very well prevent people from using taxpayer dollars in the Medicaid program. In this situation, insurance benefits would most likely enable the person needing care to stay in his or her home longer rather than be forced to go into a nursing home.

Partnership programs are expanding to more and more states and are still evolving. Reciprocal agreements among the states are needed so that policyholders who have plans that include partnership are not penalized if they move to another state. Often, couples or a surviving spouse may want to move closer to family members living in another state. They should not be deterred because that particular state does not have a partnership plan. Likewise, they should not be deterred if the state has a partnership plan but does not facilitate those who want to move and keep the benefits related to partnership. This is obviously an important issue if you own a partnership long-term care plan and want to move. Call your state department of insurance to find out if you will be giving up the benefits provided by a partnership plan.

As you are planning for retirement or if you are currently in retirement and it becomes evident that your savings may not be sufficient to pay for long-term care services, consider buying long-term care insurance in a partnership program (if your state has one available to you). This applies to married couples in particular because the assets you protect while one person needs long-term care are preserved for the surviving spouse who may live much longer and need considerable assets to meet their daily living needs as well as long-term care needs in the future. If you are single, owning long-term care insurance with a partnership program will help you preserve hard-earned assets for your retirement years as well as your heirs. Additionally, you will be able to use the benefits from your long-term care plan to stay in the comfort of your own home or an assisted living facility while receiving the care that you need. Medicaid typically provides care only in a nursing home facility.

Notes & Questions:

IN CONCLUSION

WHEN YOU PURCHASE a long-term care policy, whether through a traditional long-term care policy or a linked benefit that combines life insurance or an annuity with a long-term care rider, you don't **just** own the financial benefit of the policy; you are buying the buy peace of mind that the last years of your life will be the best they can be for your loved ones and you. Long-term health care and chronic illness care is a family issue; when one person in the family needs care, the whole family is affected.

Owning insurance protection allows you to spend your hard-earned retirement dollars without worrying about running out of money. . You can take those trips, enjoy your hobbies, and spend time with the grandchildren without being concerned that a long-term health care event will drain your resources. You'll be surprised at how much freedom you will feel once you are no longer (sometimes subconsciously) worry about running out of money.

If properly designed, a long-term care insurance policy is very affordable compared to the costs of long-term care in a healthcare facility. Long-term care expenses alone can range from $6,000 to $15,000 a month depending on where you live and where you receive healthcare services. Receiving services without a long-term care plan is very expensive, with costs projected to triple within the next 20 years.

A properly designed long-term care insurance policy will provide all the resources you need to receive care at home or in an assisted-living facility, either of which is almost always preferable to living in a nursing home. Buy your policy as soon as possible (at least start looking at age 50) because you never know when your health may change and you won't qualify for coverage. Not owning long-term care insurance for your retirement years is like owning a home without fire and homeowners insurance or like owning a vehicle without automobile insurance. Imagine going to the hospital without health insurance. Even if you have resources to pay the bill out of pocket, you will have tremendous peace of mind knowing that you have transferred the financial risk!

When it comes to owning insurance protection that covers an extended health care issue or chronic illness, don't be one who says, 'coulda, woulda, shoulda'; too much is at stake. If you buy it and don't need it, you'll be glad. If you buy it and need it, you and everyone else in the family will be glad you did. None of us want the burden of paying for our healthcare to be forced upon others—a spouse, your children, or the state.

Be sure to employ the services of a qualified professional that has experience and extensive knowledge about this product. Most insurance agents know the basics, but that is not enough. Whomever you choose should be able to answer your questions, and inform you of the important issues to consider.

Long-term care insurance is a specialized area of insurance that is still evolving. In the case of the traditional long-term care policies, the 'moving parts' of the policy drive the premium. Ask your agent to explain these moving parts so that you can make the best decision possible. Discuss which features are important in a good long-term care insurance contact and which features will increase the premium without adding real value. You want to spend your money wisely, so the more you know about the product, the better you will be able to choose the benefits that will take care of your family and you.

Don't buy a policy from someone who is a 'captive' agent representing just one company. Ask agents how many companies they represent and how they determine which ones are most suitable. Also ask agents if they have the CLTC (Certified in Long-term Care) designation, a designation that is received after a thorough study course has been completed. Whenever possible, ask the agent what courses they have taken to educate themselves about long-term care insurance.

Finally, I wish to thank you for taking time to read this book, It is my sincere desire to provide useful information and to foster the educational process that is necessary in purchasing insurance that addresses chronic illness and extended health care cost. I welcome your comments, so feel free to contact me at (205) 345-7668. .... Babs

Comforting

Babs recently did a seminar at our church about retirement planning. The information she presented was so compelling that I made an appointment for my husband and me to meet with her to discuss long-term care insurance. When we began to consider the financial impact of needing long-term care services, we decided that owning long term care insurance was the right decision for us.

We want to stay in our home to receive care for as long as possible. And we want to ensure that the resources and all options stay open to us. We enjoyed working with Babs because she carefully explained all the 'moving parts' that impact the benefit and the premium. With the information she provided, we were able to decide on the best plan at a premium we are comfortable paying.

In the years since we bought long-term care insurance from Babs, we have had questions come up and have always felt comfortable calling her. Babs took time to carefully explain the product to us in the beginning and is available now whenever we have questions. That is comforting. Over the years, what began as an inquiry into long-term care insurance for retirement planning has developed into a firm friendship.

~ Elizabeth Frazier
Registered Nurse, Case Manager, Health Educator

Comparison of a $100 Daily benefit with

3% & 5% Simple growth vs a 3% & 5% Compound Growth

YEAR	3% SIMPLE	3% COMPOUND	5% SIMPLE	5% COMPOUND
1	100.00	100.00	100.00	100.00
2	103.00	103.00	105.00	105.00
3	106.00	106.09	110.00	110.25
4	109.00	109.27	115.00	115.76
5	112.00	112.55	120.00	121.55
6	115.00	115.92	125.00	127.62
7	118.00	119.40	130.00	134.00
8	121.00	122.98	135.00	140.71
9	124.00	126.67	140.00	147.74
10	127.00	130.47	145.00	155.13
11	130.00	134.39	150.00	162.88
12	133.00	138.42	155.00	171.03
13	136.00	142.27	160.00	179.58
14	139.00	146.85	165.00	188.56
15	142.00	146.85	170.00	197.99
16	145.00	151.25	175.00	207.89
17	148.00	155.79	180.00	218.28
18	151.00	160.47	185.00	229.20
19	154.00	165.28	190.00	240.66
20	157.00	170.24	195.00	252.69
21	160.00	175.35	200.00	265.32
22	163.00	180.61	205.00	278.59
23	166.00	186.02	210.00	292.52
24	169.00	191.61	215.00	307.15
25	172.00	197.35	220.00	322.50
26	175.00	203.27	225.00	338.63
27	178.00	209.37	230.00	355.56
28	181.00	215.65	235.00	373.34
29	184.00	222.12	240.00	392.01
30	187.00	228.79	245.00	411.61
31	193.00	235.65	250.00	432.19

Glossary of Important Terms

Accelerated Payment Options

These are options available at the time of purchase that shorten the payment period. At the end of the accelerated payment period the policy is considered "paid up" and no more premiums are due. The benefits provided in the plan continue until needed or the insured dies.

Activities of Daily Living (ADLs)

Normal functions of everyday living, such as bathing, dressing, eating, toileting, etc.

Adult Day Care

These are facilities that care for adults during the day, usually to give relief to caregivers or to allow caregivers to continue working at their jobs while their loved one is being supervised.

Alternate Plan of Care

This feature provides for a plan of care that allows you to stay in your home such as adding ramps or home modifications and medical alert systems. These plans must be mutually agreed upon by you, your physician and the insurance company.

Assisted Living Facility

Facilities that provide some individualized personal care and health care services for its residents should they be needed.

Bed Reservation Benefit

This benefit pays the cost of reserving your bed in a care facility should you need to be hospitalized and expect to return to the care facility.

Benefit Period

The maximum time that a policy will pay the benefit once you qualify for a claim. This is usually measured by a dollar amount. The benefit can be paid out based on a monthly or daily reimbursement or a daily or monthly cash amount that is paid regardless of the expenses incurred.

Benefit Triggers

Requirements the policy holder must meet to be eligible to receive the benefits. Typically, the policy holder must be unable to perform 2 of 6 ADLs or suffer from a cognitive impairment such as Alzheimer's disease or dementia.

Calendar Day Elimination Period

This is the period during which covered services are received, but benefits are not being paid. It starts on the day covered services are received and continues until the selected number of calendar days have passed. Some policies require that you actually receive one day of services that you pay for while others only require that it is established that you are chronically ill and unable to perform the ADLs set out in the policy. If this rider is not added you must actually pay for services to get credit toward satisfying your elimination period.

Caregiver Training

This benefit pays expenses for care giving training provided to family members or another caregiver to enable them to provide care at home.

Chronically Ill

You are unable to perform at least two ADLs for an expected period of at least ninety days due to a loss of functional capacity or you require substantial supervision to protect you from threats to health and safety due to severe cognitive impairment.

Cognitive Impairment

A deficiency in a person's short or long-term memory that puts a person at risk.

Contingent Nonforfeiture Benefit

Included in your policy; this benefit protects you if you lapse your policy due to a substantial premium increase. You have the right within 120 days of the new premium due date, to either reduce your policy benefits so that your premium payments are not increased, or to convert your coverage to a shortened benefit period, under which no further payments are due.

Daily Benefit

The dollar amount you selected paid out on a daily or monthly basis.

Elimination Period (Deductible)

The period of time before the insurance company will begin to pay benefits; the longer the elimination period the lower the premium. In most contracts, the elimination period has to be satisfied only once.

Guaranteed Purchase Option (or Guaranteed Increase Option)

This option allows the policy holder to increase the coverage amount on a specified anniversary of the policy date and pay the corresponding increase in premium.

Guaranteed Renewable

Insurance companies can not cancel or make changes to your policy if you make timely payments of the premium. They have to renew your policy annually. The premiums are not guaranteed to remain the same as the original purchase amount. Insurance companies can raise the rates by filing a request with the department of insurance in your state.

Home Health Care

Medical and nonmedical services provided in your home. These services may include homemaker services like light housekeeping and some meal preparation, and assistance with activities of daily living, etc.

Indemnity Policy

Benefits are paid regardless of the expenses incurred. This benefit reduces the record keeping commonly associated with reimbursement policies where the actual expenses are reimbursed to the policy holder or the care provider.

Inflation Protection

This benefit is added to most policies so that the benefit selected will automatically increase every year to keep up with the expected increases in the cost of the services provided. You usually have the option of choosing between 5% simple and 3% compound inflation. Although some contracts allow for the choice of a 5% compound, it has become significantly more expensive. The choice of 5% simple will add 5% each year to the original amount selected and 3% compound will add 3% to the previous years' benefit.

Lapse Designee or Third Party Notice

This benefit allows you to name someone to receive a notice if you fail to pay the premium in a timely manner. This option is a part of the application because long-term care insurance covers dementia and Alzheimer's disease.

Licensed Health Care Practitioner

A physician, registered nurse, licensed social worker or any other individual who meets the licensing requirements.

National Association of Insurance Commissioners (NAIC)

The organization of state insurance commissioners

Nonforfeiture Benefits

If you stop paying premiums after the third year, this benefit keeps your policy in force with a reduced policy limit equal to the premiums that were paid into the policy.

Premium Modes

You can pay premiums monthly, quarterly, semi-annually or annually and this may be done by bank draft. Paying annually saves about 8% in premium each year when compared to the monthly bank draft.

Portability

Your coverage can be used anywhere in the United States.

Respite care

This is a benefit to help relieve family or other informal caregivers and is available every year for the number of days stated in the contract. Oftentimes the respite is available during the elimination period.

Return of Premium Option

Premiums used are refunded at the death of the policy holder. Some contracts will refund the premiums irrespective of the benefits that were used and others will refund premiums minus the benefits used. This option adds significant premium.

Severe Cognitive Impairment

This is a deterioration or loss in intellectual capacity that places you in jeopardy of harming yourself or others.

Shared Care Rider

A couple shares a total benefit amount and each person may access the others' benefit. When one person dies the remaining benefit, if any, is added to that of the surviving spouse.

Survivorship Option

In general, if a married couple have this added to their policy and keep the coverage in force for at least 10 years and one of them dies the surviving spouses' policy is considered "paid up" and no more premiums are due. The benefits continue to grow if inflation protection is part of the policy.

Underwriting

The process used by the insurance company to approve or reject an applicant. In most cases the process includes getting medical records, conducting a phone interview and at certain ages conducting a face to face interview.

Waiver of Premium

This is the provision for suspending premiums while the benefits are being paid.

ABOUT THE AUTHOR

 **Babs Welch Hart**, MDRT, CLTC, is president of The Hart Insurance Group, Inc.; a company built on the principles and ideals of service that she learned from her father, Stewart W. Welch, Jr., a veteran of the insurance industry. Welch is still serving clients and is at the office every weekday and often on Saturdays. In September of this year (2015) he will turn ninety-seven.

Hart began her career 22 years ago when long-term care insurance was in its infancy and considers this insurance protection for families the most significant product to be introduced by the insurance industry in the last 40 years. Why 40 years? It has been over the last 40 years that we have evolved into a nation where two income families are the norm. There is not a caregiver at home to look after the needs of elderly parents. Because of career demands, siblings are spread out in different parts of the country which means care giving is done by long distance or by the sibling that lives nearby.

Rising health care cost and shrinking government assistance have given birth to the need for long-term health care solutions. Babs Hart has published over 35 articles including an articles published in Financial Planning Magazine and

Bloomberg Business. She contributed a regular column to The Business Ink for over three years, and has done numerous educational seminars for the general public. Hart serves in an advisory capacity to Financial Planners, Wealth Managers, CPA firms and attorneys on estate planning issues. She has developed a course approved by the State of Alabama on Long-term Health Care for continuing education credit.

Hart has been a member of the International Association of Financial Planners (1998-1999) and served as its vice president for two consecutive years. In 1998, she was appointed by the governor of Alabama to the Alabama Women's Commission which studies issues important to women and makes recommendations to the legislature. She is a member of the Million dollar Round table which is the insurance industry's premier association that recognizes a high level of production and client service and represents less than 1% of the world's financial services professionals. Babs Hart lives with her husband, Robert, in Tuscaloosa, Alabama. They recently celebrated their 43rd wedding anniversary. They have three adult children, Lauren, Robert III, and Olivia.

Those are important questions, but more important:
What are your questions?: Write them down here and
then contact Babs at HartInsurancGroup.com

FOR MORE INFORMATION ABOUT
LONG-TERM CARE COSTS

If you would like to receive the most up-to-date information about the cost of Long-Term Care please visit HartInsuranceGroup.com. or call Babs at 205-345-7668.

-

We will provide you with the most up-to-date resources and reports, State-by-State, regarding the current costs of Long-Term Care.

Made in United States
Orlando, FL
13 February 2024

43623894R00072